WINDERMERE

62888

WINDERMERE

John Morrison

FRANCES LINCOLN LIMITED
PUBLISHERS

Dedicated to my dad, a down-to-earth Yorkshire patrician, who passed on his love of the Lake District.

Frances Lincoln Limited
4 Torriano Mews
Torriano Avenue
London NW5 2RZ
www.franceslincoln.com

First Frances Lincoln edition: 2009

British Library Cataloguing in Publication data
A catalogue record for this book is available from the British Library.

ISBN: 978-0-7112-2869-6

Printed and bound in Singapore

9 8 7 6 5 4 3 2 1

John Morrison can be contacted by email: hurlmere@btinternet.com
Website: www.northpix.co.uk

HALF TITLE
A misty afternoon on the lake, with a passenger cruiser about to dock at Waterhead.

TITLE PAGE
Warm evening light, still water and a sky of unclouded blue.

RIGHT
Angling and tai chi: the Windermere biathlon.

CONTENTS

INTRODUCTION

In the summer of 1930, aged just twenty-three, Alfred Wainwright made his first visit to the Lake District. Born and raised in the Lancashire milltown of Blackburn, he was unprepared for what he found when he left the train at Windermere station. 'That week changed my life,' he wrote years later. 'It was the first time that I'd looked upon beauty.'

Wainwright's moment of epiphany came when he viewed Lake Windermere from the vantage point of Orrest Head. 'I walked uphill and, as though a curtain had dramatically been torn aside, beheld a truly magnificent view. It was a moment of magic, a revelation so unexpected that I stood transfixed, unable to believe my eyes. Those few hours on Orrest Head left a spell that changed my life.'

In the years that followed, Wainwright got to know the Lake District rather better, of course, as he wrote his seven trailblazing *Pictorial Guides to the Lakeland Fells*. For all his celebrated grumpiness, Wainwright was a good judge of a view, and he never forgot that first sight of Windermere from Orrest Head.

There can be few vantage points which offer such a splendid reward for such little effort. It takes just twenty minutes to walk from the railway station, through woodland and up to the rocky outcrop of Orrest Head. And what a view it is: England's longest lake, cradled by hills, with the sands of Morecambe Bay glistening on the southern horizon, and, to the north, the craggy peaks of central Lakeland.

Millions of people have followed in Wainwright's footsteps.

The view from Orrest Head that so captivated Alfred Wainwright on his first visit to Lakeland.

A divergence of views from the top of Latterbarrow, looking over the lake towards Ambleside.

Three words that chill the blood: Family Fun Day. A crowd gathers on the Glebe in Bowness to welcome the Red Arrows display team.

Indeed, for a lot of people, Windermere *is* the Lake District. Though some visitors arrive by train, as Wainwright did, most arrive by car. And many of them get no further than Bowness, where the tea shops, ice cream parlours and a stroll around Bowness Bay prove too great a temptation. On a sunny Bank Holiday you'd need to love mankind with an unnatural intensity to want to spend much time in these Lakeland 'honeypots'. But even when Ambleside, Bowness, Windermere and Lakeside are heaving with visitors, there's still room to roam – on the shoreline, on the lake itself and on the fells which surround it.

This book is a celebration of the lake as it is today. I have tried to capture the lake and its surroundings in many different moods: showing not just what the lake *looks* like, but what it *feels* like too.

PREVIOUS PAGES

Windermere in autumn – and a solitary sailboat – from the viewpoint of Brant Fell.

RIGHT

Three walkers enjoy a ringside seat for the sunset on the rocky outcrop of Rawlinson Nab.

ABOVE

Tern is not actually a 'steamer' any longer; that's not smoke coming out of the funnel, just clouds.

LEFT

Swan, built in 1936, makes stately progress through the glassy waters.

ABOVE
Angular branches frame Storrs Temple, built in 1804 to commemorate British naval victories.

RIGHT
A couple of conifers silhouetted against a winter sky, near School Knott Tarn.

ABOVE
Blackwell, designed by Mackay Hugh Baillie Scott and completed in 1900, is one of the finest houses from the 'Arts and Crafts' movement, which it illustrates in both its interior design and architecture. It stands in a commanding position on the eastern shores of Windermere.

RIGHT
Townend, a handsome statesman's house in Troutbeck, was built in 1626 for yeoman farmer, George Browne, and is now in the care of the National Trust.

Not my dog, but she posed anyway, on the rocks at Brant Fell.

LEFT
Yachts in formation, bearing down on a defenseless photographer in a rowing boat.

ABOVE
Barely enough wind to fill the sails on a balmy summer's day.

A steamer cruises away from Waterhead, with Red Screes wearing a ten-gallon hat.

Paddling an open canoe into the bay at Waterhead.

THE LIE OF THE LAND

Windermere boasts no fells of any great height, few thundering waterfalls and, in these Silurian foothills, few rockfaces to test adventurous climbers. In fact, to hear some diehard ramblers talk, Windermere isn't really in the Lake District at all; it's just a tourist 'honeypot' with a lake attached.

Well, let them head for the higher Lakeland peaks, to tick off the 3,000ft summits. There's a lot to see around Windermere, though, in truth, a lot of visitors don't make the effort. There's a saying, among those in the tourism business, that 80 per cent of visitors go to just 20 per cent of the places. The Lakeland 'honeypots' are proof of that. Yet a few minutes after you've walked away from the hedonistic pleasures of the town, you can be out on the breezy tops, enjoying breathtaking views of the lake. Broad panoramas can be enjoyed from viewpoints such as Finsthwaite Heights, Claife Heights, Latterbarrow, Loughrigg, Gummers Howe and many others.

Wander out of the bustle of Bowness, up Helm Road to the rocky outcrop of Biskey Howe, or up Brant Fell Road to Post Knott. Both vantage points offer extensive views and an escape from the crowds. Take the carriage drive from Windermere up to Orrest Head, for the view that stopped young Alfred Wainwright in his tracks. Escape from the outdoor shops of Ambleside and explore the wooded seclusion of Stock Ghyll Beck, and its waterfall, before taking the steep path to the top of Wansfell, which, at 1,574ft/480m, is the highest of the first range of peaks which overlook Windermere.

One of those paths that beg to be explored, on Claife Heights.

This may be the best view of them all, with Windermere laid out in the landscape like a ribbon of silver. Notice how the Lakeland landscape changes: low Silurian foothills to the south, receding towards the treacherous sands of Morecambe Bay. To the north, beyond Loughrigg Fell, are the higher hills, the Borrowdale Volcanics: Fairfield, Dollywagon Pike and the distinctive double silhouette of the Langdale Pikes. The view was familiar to William Wordsworth: 'In the Vale of Windermere, if a spectator looks for gentle and lovely scenes, the eye is turned to the South; if for the grand, towards the North.'

Turn around to see The Hundreds: common pasture land which was divided up in the seventeenth century, and the grazing rights granted to the yeoman farmers of Troutbeck. Town End, the characterful home of George Browne, is due east of Wansfell, in Troutbeck village. The house, sensitively restored, is now owned by the National Trust and open to the public.

To the north the brown fells are divided up by drystone walls – some acting as 'funnels' to gather the sheep off the higher fells. The narrow road in the middle distance is 'The Struggle', the old road from Ambleside that climbs up, up, up to the top of Kirkstone Pass – a struggle indeed! – where a white building, from here seeming no bigger than a grain of salt, is actually one of England's highest pubs, the Kirkstone Pass Inn.

Windermere is an intriguing mixture of the natural and the man-made, with many 'improvements' having been made to the landscape in recent centuries. It is arguably the most artificially enhanced valley in the Lake District: a garden with a lake as its centrepiece. After the Enclosure Acts of the eighteenth and nineteenth centuries, a lot of common land and open pasture was brought into private ownership, and the new landowners were keen to make their mark on the landscape. They had a vision of how they wanted the lake to look – a rural arcadia, no less – and if it didn't match their expectations they were quite prepared to alter the lie of the land.

The eastern and western shores of the lake present a startling contrast. Most of the eastern shore is in private hands. Houses with lake frontage present an impenetrable barrier to anyone wanting access to the shore. Though the A591 hugs the contours of the lake, you can drive from Waterhead to Newby Bridge without seeing more than a few tantalising glimpses of water. Thankfully, much of the western shoreline of the lake is accessible to walkers.

The view across the lake from Wansfell is dominated by the wooded slopes of Claife Heights – in places, all the way down to the water's edge – with Wetherlam and the Coniston range as a backdrop. For centuries the woodlands were cleared to create sheep pasture; when William Wordsworth was born, in 1770, these fells would have been almost bare of trees. Claife Heights, previously classified as common land, were bought and enclosed by John Curwen, who had made his home on Belle Isle. He planted larch trees – 30,000 of them – mostly for aesthetic reasons. Other landowners followed his example, helping to create the gently wooded aspect which now typifies the lake and its immediate surroundings.

The breezy summit of Wansfell, looking over Ambleside to Loughrigg Fell.

Conifers reflected in the still waters of High Dam, built to provide the motive power for Stott Park Bobbin Mill.

Such 'improvements' were not to everyone's taste. William Wordsworth complained about the conifer plantations, which 'caused great injury to the appearance of the country'. But then, after producing acres of blank verse, not approving of things was his forté. He even found fault with the local tradition of whitewashing houses, because they stood out too prominently in the landscape.

It's tempting to look back a couple of centuries and, through the distorting mirror of time, see Windermere as a rural idyll, unspoiled by industry. The facts are rather different. Mills, forges and ironworks were built wherever there was enough water to turn a waterwheel, albeit on a smaller scale than in the towns. There was even a gunpowder factory at the southern end of the lake.

Broadleaved trees were planted, in addition to the stands of conifers: principally birch, oak and hazel. They were coppiced – cut back every ten to fifteen years – to provide the raw materals for an important local industry. Wooden bobbins were needed in huge quantities by the Lancashire cotton mills. At the height of the industry there were more than sixty bobbin mills in South Lakeland. Fast-flowing rivers and streams – including Cunsey Beck and Stock Ghyll Beck – were dammed and diverted, confined and culverted, to provide the motive power. An original waterwheel can still be seen in the middle of Ambleside, where Stock Ghyll Beck flows through the town. The last bobbin mill – at Stott Park, near Lakeside – was saved from extinction by the National Park Authority, and is open to the public as a working museum.

The River Leven, flowing swiftly through the Backbarrow Gorge to the south of Newby Bridge, was the site of heaviest industry. To maintain a good head of water, a long weir was built across the river near the Swan Inn. The first blast furnace in the north of England was built at Backbarrow. Close by, a cotton mill was converted, in 1895, to make Dolly Blue: an additive used when washing clothes to make the whites look even whiter. It was a surreal scene. The factory was blue, the surroundings were blue; at the end of their shift, the workers were blue (the company laid on their own bus for those who lived in Ulverston). The building is now a hotel and timeshare complex.

At 11 miles/17km, Windermere is the longest lake in England, and, with a maximum depth of 196ft/60m, is our second deepest lake; only Wastwater is deeper. The shallowest area is around Bowness Bay; at its broadest point – between Low Wood and Pull Wyke – the lake is more than a mile wide.

There are fourteen well-wooded islands dotted around the lake, plus a few more which appear and disappear depending on the water level. Though the lake isn't tidal, the level can rise quickly after heavy rain in the lake's catchment area to the north. A drop of water entering the lake via the rivers Rothay or Brathay will take a full nine months to drain into the River Leven, which very soon broadens into a sandy estuary as it enters Morecambe Bay.

The largest island, opposite Bowness Bay, is Belle Isle, originally called Long Holme. It is so long that it almost divides the lake in two. In 1774 Thomas English built the round house on Belle Isle – an architectural curiosity – though William Gell, writing in 1797, wasn't impressed. 'It wants only a little green paint and a label of Souchong or fine Hyson to make it exactly like a large shop tea canister.' Long Holme became Belle Isle when it was bought by John Curwen, in 1789, as a wedding present for his wife, Isabella. Gell also lamented the fact that there weren't more boats to be seen on the lake: a problem that has been solved in recent years!

LEFT

A hidden gem: the little, low, roughcast sixteenth-century church of St Anthony at Cartmel Fell.

BELOW

The family pews – and the triple decker pulpit – inside St Anthony's church.

RIGHT
A section of the old road – still paved near Belle Grange – between Kendal and Hawkshead.

BELOW
Mossy woodland on Claife Heights, overlooking the lake's western shore.

LEFT

Learning to sail on a placid lake, with the familiar outline of the Langdale Pikes in the background.

BELOW

Boats at their moorings: reflections in still water.

The view north from Wansfell – the land divided up by a patchwork of drystone walls.

LEFT

A fell-runner stops to check her map on Loughrigg Fell, with Ill Bell in the distance

TOP

A hardy Herdwick sheep – the presiding spirit of the Lakeland fells.

ABOVE

Ears, tongue, tail and all four legs at full extension, on the walk up to Gummer's How.

A tranquil mooring in a sheltered bay
at the northern end of the lake.

A shaft of light penetrates the gloom to pick out a solitary sailboat.

The new marina in front of the Low Wood Hotel.

The Old Post Office, in Winster, has a datestone of 1600.

THE FIRST VISITORS

As strange as it may seem to us today, it's really only during the last 250 years that people have visited the Lake District in any numbers. It wasn't on the way to anywhere; it was barely on the map. It was viewed with suspicion as a remote region of precipitous peaks and impassable roads.

Apart from free spirits such as Celia Feinnes and Daniel Defoe, the Lake District mountains held little interest to those who did not earn their living here. Working people had neither the time nor the means to travel, of course, while those of nobler birth looked further afield. Defoe, more at home on the cobbled streets of London, found Westmorland 'the wildest, most barren and frightful of any country I have passed over in England.'

During the early years of the eighteenth century, young men of wealth and breeding went on the Grand Tour of Europe. In the Alps and the Dolomites they found the epitome of the sublime and the picturesque. They returned with an appreciation of Palladian architecture, French chateaux, and the landscape paintings of Nicolas Poussin and Claude Lorrain . . . and maybe, like William Wordsworth, sowed their wild oats too.

Ironically, it was war in Europe that opened up the Lake District. When their travels were interrupted by the French Revolution and the Napoleonic Wars, these well-heeled sightseers were forced to look closer to home: the Scottish Highlands, Snowdonia and the Lake District. With improvements in the road networks – and the development of turnpikes – visitors started coming from about 1750, the beginning of the Romantic movement. It was quite an adventure, undertaken by pioneers. The poet Thomas Gray expected to be overwhelmed by the grandeur of the Lakeland landscape, and he wasn't disappointed.

The first guidebooks, published from 1770 onwards, painted the Lake District as a threatening place. Nature was romantic, yet terrifying. In the imagination of these first adventurers, waterfalls became awesome cataracts. A steep slope was a precipice. Mountain were vertiginous peaks, dwarfing the diminutive figures who stood in their shadows. If they could no longer visit the Alps, the visitors would do the next best thing . . . recreate the Alpine landscape in the north-west corner of England.

The next wave of visitors came to be awed, frightened, overwhemed, amazed and amused, but they didn't want to exert themselves or get out of breath. They were tourists rather than adventurers. Instead of discovering the beauties of Lakeland for themselves, they were happier to stay in their carriages until the guide told them they had reached the next picturesque view.

In 1778 Thomas West published his *Guide to the Lakes*, listing the best 'stations and viewpoints', from which visitors could appreciate the formal qualities of the landscape. These stations weren't just points printed on a map; they existed on the ground as well. At Claife Station, for example, above the western shore of Windermere, was a lodge commanding fine views across the lake.

Visitors could enjoy the views by looking through the bow windows in the drawing room. In an effort to 'improve' on Nature, and imitate seasonal changes, each pane of glass was a different colour. Light green glass represented spring, yellow was for summer and orange for autumn, while light blue gave the scene the chilly hues of winter. A dark blue window bathed the scene in 'moonlight'; another had a lilac tinge to suggest a thunderstorm.

Though only a short walk from Ambleside, Loughrigg Fell offers a tantalising taste of wilder country.

Hill Top, the former home of Beatrix Potter, is a popular attraction . . . especially for Japanese visitors. It now ranks as the most popular National Trust property in the Lakes.

The lodge still stands, though in a ruinous state. Other viewing stations around Windermere were to be found at both the north and south tips of Belle Isle (with no public access today), Queen Adelaide's Hill, and Brant Fell near Bowness. Above Robin Lane, the old road between Ambleside and Troutbeck, is a small stone structure: not merely another cairn, but a viewing station. Visitors could stand here, admire the view and have somewhere to rest their copy of West's book – open at the appropriate page, of course.

William Gilpin wrote his *Lake District Guide* (full title: *Observations, relative chiefly to Picturesque Beauty, made in the year 1772 on several parts of England, particularly the Mountains and Lakes of Cumberland and Westmorland*). He rhapsodised about the aesthetics of the Lakeland landscape, pointing out those elements which created an effect he called 'picturesque'.

Gilpin looked at Windermere as though it was a picture in a gallery, and his rules were both specific and prescriptive. Nature tried her best, but, on the whole, Gilpin preferred the Lakeland landscape when re-imagined on canvas. Paintings and engravings of the period showed Italian gondolas gliding serenely across the lake: a typical flight of fancy.

He encouraged his readers to turn their back on the landscape – quite literally – and view it via a convex mirror. This device, known as a 'Claude glass,' created a sepia-toned image resembling the paintings of Claude Lorrain – one of many artists who attempted to improve on nature by infusing it with drama and romance. If these notions sound rather odd today, be assured that Gilpin would recognise, in a lot of landscape photography, many of his ideas about composition.

Articles appeared in society magazines, extolling the Lakeland scenery. The Lakeland tour began to take shape, with pre-selected itineraries for the visitors, who became known, rather disparagingly, as 'Lakers'. Then, as now, visitors wanted expansive views while expending the minimum of effort, with, ideally, a welcoming hostelry close at hand. Their passions and preoccupations laid them open to mockery. In 1868 John Wilson wrote: 'How the owls of Windermere must laugh at the silly Lakers, that under the garish eye of day, enveloped in clouds of dust, whirl along in rattling post-shays in pursuit of the picturesque!'

Windermere was, from the beginning, an important port of call on the Lakeland tour. Regular stage-coach services brought visitors along the turnpike roads to coaching inns such as The Salutation in Ambleside, The Swan at Newby Bridge and The Wild Boar Hotel, near Crook.

Wordsworth lived in Rydal Mount from 1814 until his death in 1850. He kept a jaundiced eye on the visitors, and didn't much like what he saw. He didn't think the tourists would benefit – 'mentally or morally', as he put it – from a closer acquaintance with his beloved lakes. Nevertheless, the poet found time to produce his own guidebook to the Lakes, aimed at these same tourists. He was one of the first writers (though certainly not the last) to complain about the influx of visitors to the Lake District, while taking their money for his books.

The book was quite a hit, dwarfing the sales of his poetry. There's a story (it may be apocryphal, but I'd like to think it's true) that a clergyman once asked Wordsworth if he'd written anything else. The story makes no mention of Wordsworth's reply, but you can almost hear him spluttering!

ABOVE

Steaming along past Wray Bay.

LEFT

Steam launch *Souvenir d'Antan* making graceful progress across the lake.

ABOVE
An enviable location: a house, a boathouse and a garden that extends down to the lake.

RIGHT
More exclusive homes in the Storrs area, just south of Bowness.

ABOVE

Storm clouds gather behind Low Wood Marina.

RIGHT

Boats and apartments at the Windermere Marina Village, near Ferry Nab.

ABOVE
Hazy light on the lake, from the lofty viewpoint of Loughrigg Fell.

LEFT
A fly fisherman casts his line on Ghyll Head Reservoir.

TOP

The roads on the western side of the lake see much less traffic than those on the eastern side.

ABOVE

Autumn colours by the River Brathay at Clappersgate.

Rydal Water, and the River Rothay, draining into a distant Windermere.

LEFT ABOVE

The whole of the lake can be seen from the top of Wansfell.

LEFT BELOW

Belle Isle, almost dividing the lake in two, seen from Claife Heights.

BELOW

Swans mate for life, so I'm told; appropriately this pair seem to be making the shape of a heart.

ABOVE

The boathouse of Wray Castle is as eccentric as the mansion itself.

RIGHT

Great light – but not much wind – for a windsurfer.

ABOVE
Dinghies for hire, pulled up on to the beach at Waterhead.

RIGHT
The sheltered waters of the River Leven are a playground for boats big and small.

ABOVE
Messing about in boats on the River Leven at Newby Bridge.

RIGHT
Evening comes to Bowness Bay, with the passenger cruisers moored for the night.

Piers and boathouses line the eastern shoreline of the lake.

42085
51
A
SC

THE RAILWAY ERA

Stage-coach travel was too expensive for working people; the era of cheap travel really began in 1847, with the opening of the Windermere Railway. The 1840s was the decade of 'railway mania', and the original plan was to run a spur from the main Lancaster–Carlisle line at Oxenholme, through Kendal, to meet the lake at Low Wood. The line would continue to Ambleside, Keswick and beyond.

Wordsworth's wasn't the only voice to be raised in protest, but his was the most famous. He lamented, in the strongest terms, that 'the imperfectly educated classes are not likely to draw much good from rare visits to the lakes', and reiterated his fears in a sonnet he sent to the *Morning Post*.

His advice to these 'uneducated persons' was unequivocal. 'Go to a pantomime, a farce, or a puppet show, if you want noisy pleasure . . . but may those who have given proof that they prefer other gratifications continue to be safe from the molestations of cheap trains pouring out their hundreds at a time along the margin of Windermere.'

Cornelius Nicholson, the railway's most prominent sponsor, had other ideas, hoping to 'give the Lake District the full benefits of railway communication' for a ticket-buying public. The outcome was a compromise; the railway line was laid from Oxenholme to the unassuming village of Birthwaite, and, despite the best efforts of the railway lobby in subsequent years, was never extended.

Tourists came to see Windermere; they didn't want to get off the train at a place called Birthwaite, which, in any case, was a mile and a half from the lake. Canny locals changed the name of the station – and the village itself – to 'Windermere' (there being, at the time, no Trades Description Act to worry about).

A steam-hauled train, heading for Lakeside, on the Lakeside–Haverthwaite Railway.

Cheap tickets – and special 'excusion' trains – opened up the Lake District to working people. In the first year of operation, the line carried 120,000 passengers. In his dotage, Wordsworth fumed. He liked to see peasants toiling in the fields; they added scale and a little local colour to the Lakeland scene. But if all the world's a stage, he preferred his yokels to have non-speaking roles. All he really approved of was the literary gentility: men of lofty ideals, who nevertheless lived the simple life. Men, that is, like himself.

The Windermere Hotel welcomed the first arrivals by train, to be followed by other hotels, lodgings and public houses. The town expanded rapidly, spilling downhill towards Bowness and the lake. Windermere remains the only town within the National Park to be served by the railway.

Wordsworth was scathing, too, about the new industrialists who, having made their piles from the cotton mills of Lancashire and the woollen mills of West Yorkshire, built rural retreats by the lake. One of the finest is Belsfield (now a hotel), a prominent mansion overlooking Bowness Bay. Built for Baroness de Sternberg, Belsfield became the home of Henry William Schneider, chairman of the Barrow Shipyard.

Schneider began every working day by strolling down to the lake, followed – at a respectful distance – by a butler carrying his breakfast on a tray. Schneider boarded his steam yacht, the *Esperance*, and enjoyed a leisurely breakfast afloat, as his crew delivered him to Lakeside, at the southern end of the lake. Schneider transferred to a private carriage on the Furness Railway – of which he was a director – for the scenic route along the coast to his office in Barrow-in-Furness. Now *that* is commuting . . .

The attractions of lakeside living encouraged other wealthy people to build houses – mostly as holiday and retirement homes. Brathay Hall, near Ambleside, was built in 1788; it is now

A passenger cruiser passes the façade of Storrs Hall Hotel.

a centre for outdoor pursuits. Two years later, Storrs Hall was built on a prime, south-facing site, on a wooded promontory, with wonderful views down the lake. The mansion later became the residence of Colonel John Bolton, a Liverpool ship-owner, slave trafficker and patron of the Windermere Regattas. Colonel Bolton, a staunch patriot, created the octagonal Temple of Heroes, in 1804. Jutting out into the lake, the temple was joined to his land by a stone causeway. It celebrates the careers of four Admirals – Nelson, Howe, Vincent and Duncan – and the naval victories of the Napoleonic Wars. Bolton's role in the slave trade paints Storrs Hall in a rather different light; the hall is now – like so many of these grandiose buildings – a hotel.

While some of these houses fit their surroundings, others stick out like the proverbial sore thumb. Imagine a castle drawn by a seven-year-old child, and imagine an architect using this drawing as a blueprint. Actually, there's no real need to imagine it, because it exists: Wray Castle, a preposterous, mock-medieval folly – complete with battlements and arrowslits – was built in the 1840s for James Dyson, a retired surgeon from Liverpool. Both incongruous and anachronistic, Wray Castle was nevertheless one of the few buildings around the lake to get William Wordsworth's seal of approval.

Brockhole was built in 1899 for industrialist William Henry Gaddum, with lawns and terraced gardens extending down to the lake. In 1966 the mansion was bought by the National Park Authority and became the Lake District Visitor Centre. Blackwell, built by Manchester brewer Sir Edward Holt to designs by Mackay Hugh Baillie Scott at the turn of the nineteenth century, is a superb example of the Arts and Crafts movement both in its architecture and interior design. It is now owned and managed by the Lakeland Arts Trust, and is also open to the public.

Wordsworth lived just long enough to see his worst fears realised, though he probably never imagined – even in his nightmares – just how many people would throng to the Lake District. Or that most of them would arrive by car. Or that

The battlements of Wray Castle rise incongruously from the woodland on the western shore.

they would attach a touring caravan and bring traffic on narrow Lakeland roads to a virtual standstill. The start of the conservation movement can be traced back to Wordsworth's opposition to the Windermere railway. The battle was half-won, in that Windermere was as far into the Lake District as the railway ever penetrated. But Wordsworth, and others, realised that there were many other battles that would need to be fought – and won – if the Lake District was to retain its unique character. John Ruskin and Canon Rawnsley helped to set up the Lake District Defense Assocation: a forerunner of the National Trust, which was established in 1895.

Wordsworth's big idea, in landscape terms, was to envisage the Lake District as 'a sort of national property in which every man has a right and interest who has an eye to perceive and a heart to enjoy'. That's the national park ethos in a nutshell, though we had to wait until 1951 for 885 square miles/ 2,292sq km of the Lake District to be designated as the largest of the twelve National Parks in England and Wales.

A lot of land around Windermere is looked after by the National Trust – including Town End, a wonderfully evocative seventeenth-century house in Troutbeck; Fell Foot Park at the southern end of the lake; the gothic ghastliness that is Wray Castle; and four miles of the western lake shore between Ash Landing and Low Wray Bay. Beatrix Potter left her home, Hill Top in Near Sawrey, to the National Trust, along with the many other properties she had aquired with the royalties from sales of her children's books around the world.

The battle is ongoing for the heart and soul of the Lake District, and the pressures on Windermere, in particular, are immense. The National Park Authority has the unenviable task of balancing the needs of locals and visitors, commercial interests and conservationists. If inappropriate developments are allowed to proliferate unchecked, then Windermere could become a rural shopping mall. If tourists keep flocking to the same Lakeland 'honeypots' in ever increasing numbers, the danger is that they will destroy what it was they came to see.

Once there were sixty bobbin mills in South Lakeland; the last one – Stott Park, near Lakeside – is now a working museum.

Springtime daffodils in the churchyard
of Jesus Church, in Troutbeck.

A swan glides between Storrs Temple and its reflection.

A sunset transforms a swan into a silhouette and the water into liquid gold.

A string of Christmas lights, hung from bare branches at Waterhead.

ABOVE

Preparing for a day's sailing in the marina at Bowness.

RIGHT

Three canoes lashed together, a makeshift sail and a day these youngsters will remember for a long time.

Safe mooring in a quiet bay near Ferry House.

RIGHT

The Drunken Duck, near Ambleside: good food, real ale and breathtaking views from the beer garden.

BELOW

A pint of bitter at The Brown Horse in Winster.

LEFT
Good times: a hot summer's day and an inflatable dinghy.

BELOW
Navigating the River Brathay beneath the bridge at Clappersgate.

Loughrigg Fell offers easy walking, and a bewildering network of good paths.

A golden labrador leads the way across Loughrigg Fell, with the bulk of Fairfield on the horizon.

BOWNESS AND AMBLESIDE

The Bowness of today (with its Sunday-best name of Bowness-on-Windermere) has cheerfully dedicated itself to parting visitors from their hard-earned cash. Before the arrival of the railway, however, Bowness was just a tight knot of houses grouped around the fifteenth-century parish church, dedicated to St Martin.

While Bowness can boast more old houses than Windermere – the Hole in the Wall pub, for example, dates back to 1612 – it too is essentially a Victorian invention. One of the prime movers behind the town's expansion was William Henry Schneider. Having transformed Barrow-in-Furness from a village into an industrial powerhouse, he turned his attention to his adopted home town.

Windermere had the name, but Bowness had the lake itself, and quickly grew into what was essentially an inland resort. The Hydro Hotel was built in 1881 to cater for wealthy hypochondriacs who wanted to take the waters. They could follow a path behind the hotel up to the rocky outcrop of Biskey Howe, to enjoy a panoramic view of the lake. They could stroll through a park, known as the Glebe, to the wooded promontory of Cockshott Point, and socialise along the promenade around the bay, which was created in 1912.

Why do people flock to Bowness in such numbers? Well, we're creatures of habit. We may rebel against our parents in so many ways, but when we're planning a day out, our default option is to take our children where our parents took us. The shops, pubs and tea-rooms of Bowness are the beneficiaries of this collective lack of imagination. The best of Bowness is the bay itself – with its piers, boatmens' huts and the constant to-ing and fro-ing of the cruisers and steamers. To see the lake in a different light, buy a return ticket to Ambleside or Lakeside; if you can travel in *Tern*, a steamer that's well over 100 years old, so much the better.

The Romans knew Ambleside – not as a holiday destination, of course, but as a garrison – and they knew it as Galava. They built their camp around AD 100 on a floodplain at the northern end of the lake, near the confluence of the rivers Brathay and Rothay – creating a raised platform to lift the camp clear of high water. The Romans had piers nearby, and no doubt used the lake both for carrying goods and for recreation.

Here, at the northen extremity of the Roman empire, 500 sun-loving Italian legionaires would watch the rain hammer down and dream of home. Galava was occupied for about 250 long years. The foundations can still be seen, in Borrans Park, though you'll need a good imagination to reconstruct the camp in your mind's eye.

If Keswick is the 'capital' of the northern lakes, Ambleside serves a similar role in South Lakeland. And, like Keswick, it has the most wonderful setting, cradled by hills. The market town expanded, from the middle of the nineteenth century, on the expectation that the Oxenholme–Windermere line would be extended. It never was, though Ambleside seems to manage perfectly well without it.

Bowness marina, backed up by Belle Isle and more darkening skies.

63639
Odyssey
MOJO
63246
Sweet Talker
La Jable

You might think that people come to the Lake District precisely to get away from rampant consumerism. You *might* think that . . . but you'd be wrong. Yes, there are people who disappear over the first horizon with little more than a home-made cheese and pickle sandwich, but they are outnumbered – round here, at least – by those who just want to carry on shopping in a pleasant, semi-rural environment. While Bowness deals in souvenirs, Ambleside's speciality is outdoor clothing. When any shop closes, it tends to re-open as yet another outlet for walking boots, breathable cagoules and 'three-season' sleeping bags.

The most famous building in Ambleside – certainly the most photographed – is also the smallest. Bridge House stands on a bridge that spans Stock Beck. It wasn't built by a Scotsman to avoid land tax, as some have suggested. It was actually an apple store attached to Ambleside Hall. Today it is a diminutive outpost of the National Trust.

Ambleside, like Windermere town, keeps its distance from the lake. The town's waterfront is Waterhead: a smaller, less crowded version of Bowness Bay. Once the Windermere Steam Yacht Company created the steamer pier, in 1845, Waterhead thrived. Ambleside Youth Hostel vies with the Wateredge Inn for the prime position, overlooking the lake. The hotel wins, because of its beer garden, which extends right down to the water.

A couple of smart cruisers moored at the piers of Waterhead, as the sun goes down.

ABOVE

One of the few lakeside dwellings which incorporates a boathouse.

RIGHT

The Lilies of the Valley: islands lying to the west of Belle Isle.

The lake, looking south, from Robin Lane, an old drove road between Troutbeck and Ambleside.

RIGHT ABOVE

Two rivers – the Brathay and the Rothay – meet as they meander into Windermere.

RIGHT BELOW

A farming landscape: the view north from Orrest Head.

LEFT

A black headed gull telling a joke to another gull, who's heard it before. A third seagull ponders the meaning of life.

BELOW

These Canada geese were *very* close (I only had a wide-angle lens on the camera as they flew past).

RIGHT

Waiting for a bite on the River Leven near Newby Bridge.

Old Town

Ethereal light from dark skies: a picture that's unlikely to appear in the tourist brochures.

The sun goes down beyond the gardens of Storrs Hall Hotel.

A view of Latterbarrow from the Low Wood Marina.

The last of the light, after the sunset has faded.

The lights of Bowness Bay reflected in the water.

ROCKING THE BOAT

The first written evidence of a ferry across Windermere dates back to 1454, with nothing in the account to suggest that this was a new venture. The ferry crossed the lake at its narrowest point, from Ferry Nab to the Ferry Inn. On one tragic night in 1635, the ferry sank with a wedding party from Hawkshead on board, killing forty-seven passengers. They were buried in a mass grave at St Martin's church in Bowness.

Another ferry ran from Millerground, on the eastern shore of the lake, to Belle Grange on the west. This route formed part of what was once the main road linking the market towns of Kendal and Hawkshead. The ferryman's house can still be seen at Millerground; a bell, in a tiny belfry on the gable end of the cottage, was rung if the ferry needed to be summoned from Belle Grange. The first steam-powered ferry was introduced in 1870. It ran on underwater cables, as the current ferry, *Mallard*, does today.

The lake has seen commercial traffic. Transporting raw materials or finished products – such as slate, sand, timber and quarried stone – would be easier and cheaper by boat or barge, rather than trying to negotiate rough and rutted tracks with horse-drawn carts.

Windermere has quite a tradition of recreational boating: not just taking to the water, but doing so in style. As long as men have sailed or rowed boats on the lake, they will have raced each another. John Curwen raced his sailing yacht, *John*, against other local worthies. Some boats were so large, and their rigging so complex, that they needed paid crewmen (often recruited from Morecambe).

The first Windermere Regatta was held in 1825, under the patronage of wealthy men such as Curwen and John Bolton, whose home, Storrs Hall, was the starting point for a flotilla of lake craft. Bolton was entertaining some literary luminaries – including William Wordsworth, poet laureate Robert Southey and Sir Walter Scott – whom he was keen to impress. An account of the event, written

Mallard, the cross-lake ferry, with the Ill Bell range beyond.

MALLARD
DANGER
KEEP CLEAR
OF
FERRY CABLES
6

A passenger steamer approaches Rawlinson Nab.

by John Lockhart, Scott's biographer, suggests that Bolton succeeded. 'Music and sunshine, flags, streamers and gay dresses, the merry hum of voices and the rapid splashing of innumerable oars, made up a dazzling mixture of sensations as the flotilla wound its way among the richly foliated islands and along bays and promontories peopled with enthusiastic spectators.'

The years that followed saw many other entertainments on the lake: yacht races, rowing competitions, spectacular firework displays, mock battles (with miniature cannons), and, once the water sports had finished, wrestling matches, tug of war contests, dancing and drinking. In attendance at the 1857 regatta was Charles Dickens, who accepted a challenge (hopefully more of a publicity stunt) from Thomas Longmire, a champion wrestler and, for a few years in the nineteenth century, landord of the Hole in the Wall pub in Bowness. These sporting occasions were the precursors of the famous Grasmere Sports.

The excitement level went up a few notches when, during the long, hard winter of 1878–9, Windermere froze solid. It was, according to a contemporary account, 'a sight worth travelling hundreds of miles' to see. Skaters danced on the ice in Bowness Bay, with musical accompaniment provided by the Windermere Volunteer Band. Sailing yachts were fitted with metal runners, so they could race on the ice.

The lake froze again in 1895 and 1917, which gave the newspapers something other than war news to write about. Old photographs show people skating on the ice, accompanied by a policeman . . . also on skates. The next big freezes were in 1929, 1946 and, the most recent occurence, 1963.

Lady of the Lake, the first steam yacht to operate on an English lake, was launched in 1845, the same year that *Great Britain*, Brunel's innovative iron steamship, sailed from Liverpool to New York in just two weeks. At 75ft/23m in length, with a long bowsprit and paddles at either side, *Lady of*

The former steamship *Tern* cruises the southern reaches of the lake.

the Lake must have been a splendid sight. Predictably, the yacht's launch was opposed by William Wordsworth.

With a draught of just 16in/40cm, *Lady of the Lake* could negotiate the shallow waters of the River Leven as far south as the quay at Newby Bridge. The Windermere Steam Yacht Company ran a regular passenger service between Newby Bridge and Ambleside. *Lady of the Lake* proved so popular with visitors that a second steamer, *Lord of the Isles*, was commssioned the following year.

The steam age brought the railway to Windermere town in 1847. A few years later, in 1868, a spur was driven from the Furness Railway to a terminus at Lakeside. The name 'Windermere' was already taken (albeit under false pretences), so passengers alighted at 'Windermere Lakeside'. Since their trains were arriving at Lakeside, it made sense for the Furness Railway Company to diversify into steamers. A quay was built, so passengers were able to continue their journey by water. This rail link allowed pleasure steamers to make a round trip, calling at Bowness and Waterhead, and linking up with trains at Lakeside: an 'integrated transport system', no less!

The first passenger steamer was *Swan* (later to be replaced by another boat of the same name). The slim, elegant *Tern* was built in 1891, and, amazingly, is still in operation today – though now she is powered by diesel. *Teal* and *Swan* (built in 1936 and 1938 respectively) completed the fleet, which is now operated by Windermere Lake Cruises. On balmy summer evenings you can hear the distinctive syncopation of trad jazz, as yet another party – stag or hen – cruises serenely down the lake.

Dr Beeching wielded his infamous axe in 1965, closing the branch line from Ulverston to Lakeside. A band of rail enthusiasts successfully re-opened a section of the line as the Lakeside and Haverthwaite Railway, and steam-hauled trains operate most days in the year for fans of very short rail journeys.

The Windermere Sailing Club was founded in 1860, in an attempt to bring a little order to the yacht races being held on the lake. Instead of having a handicap system (always an

unsatisfactory compromise), the club encouraged its members to race in boats of similar size. When a boating dispute was referred to the Royal Yachting Association, the club received this supercilious reply: 'This body has no jurisdiction over duck ponds.' Well, really! It may have been in response to this slight that the club received the royal warrant. In 1887, the year of Queen Victoria's Diamond Jubilee, the club became the Royal Windermere Yacht Club.

The races were social events, with crowds gathering on the lawns of the Ferry Hotel to eat, drink and watch the elegant 'Windermere class' yachts sailing by. Punters crowded into Bowness Bay, where the association has its clubhouse, to bet on the outcome of the races. Steam launches would follow the yachts, and announce the winner with sirens. In the early years of the nineteenth century, the length of Windermere Class sailing boats was standardised at 17ft/5m. These elegant, wooden-hulled yachts still race today: a stirring sight on Sunday afternoons.

Sir William Forwood, a prominent member of the RWYC, wrote of the lake's unpredictability. 'On Windermere nothing is certain. We may stand in to get a breeze we expect to come off the land and find ourselves headed off in the opposite direction, and we frequently see two yachts not fifty yards apart heading the same way on opposite tacks.'

The Windermere Marina, just south of Ferry Nab and the Lake Warden's office, was established in 1962. There are many other moorings for sailing boats around the lake, especially at the back of Belle Isle and in the more sheltered bays.

Some lake-users preferred raw power to the vagaries of the wind. The Windermere Motor Boat Racing Club was founded in 1925, based in a modest clubhouse in Bowness Bay. As membership increased, larger premises were needed. In 1950 the WMBRC moved into Broad Leys, a Grade 1 listed building designed in the Arts and Crafts style by Charles Voysey and built in 1898. For the next fifty years, motor boat races were a feature of every weekend from April to September, accompanied by a banshee howl as inboard and outboard engines were flogged to the limits of engineering tolerance.

The lake is a lot quieter since the 10mph speed limit on motorboats was introduced in 2005; time seems to stand still on a misty morning.

The lake has witnessed numerous attempts at water speed records, culminating in Sir Henry Seagrave's successful – but tragic – run over a measured mile in 1930. He reached a speed of 119mph before his boat, *Miss England II*, flipped over, killing both Sir Henry and his mechanic.

Speed Records Week was held annually, each October, from the 1970s onward, with records continuing to be broken. The records stopped and the noise abated on April 1 2005, when a 10mph speed limit was introduced on Windermere for all powered boats. To hear some people talk, the speed limit was brought in at short notice, on a bureaucratic whim, without due consultation. The truth is rather different.

In 1976 a speed limit was introduced on Coniston and Derwentwater, and on Ullswater five years later. In 1989 came a suggestion, from the Friends of the Lake District, that the restriction should be extended to Windermere as well. In 1991 the Lake District Special Planning Board decided to apply for a 10mph byelaw. A period of consultation was followed, in 1994, by a Public Inquiry.

The issue pitted the National Park Authority, the Friends of the Lake District and other environmental bodies against those who enjoyed – and profited from – water-sports on Windermere. Despite some misgivings about the effect that a speed restriction might have on the local ecomony, tranquility won the day. Powerboat racing was incompatible with the National Park's stated aim of promoting 'quiet recreation'. Though there isn't an outright ban on speedboats on Windermere, cruising around the lake at a stately 10mph is a bit like driving a Ferrari but never getting out of first gear.

Powerboat racers have gone elsewhere. Coniston is now the venue for Records Week, while the WMBRC race in Cavendish Dock, just outside Barrow-in-Furness: a body of water without a speed limit, but without a backdrop of Lakeland hills either. Windermere has changed. For those who had built up businesses selling speedboats and teaching watersports, it's changed for the worse. For those, like me, who prefer silence to speed, it seems that the lake has changed for the better.

Sailing past the Belsfield Hotel and the jetties of Bowness Bay.

A shaft of light, from a break in the storm clouds, illuminates boats moored behind Belle Isle.

LEFT
Looking south down the lake from the promontory of Rawlinson Nab.

ABOVE
Still life with moored boat, and the sun setting over the Coniston hills.

ABOVE
Ripples disturb a placid lake as the light fades.

RIGHT
A few seconds of sunlight, with clouds descending over the hills at the northern end of the lake.

FOLLOWING PAGES
Queen of the Lake, one of the classic passenger launches on the lake.

Princess of the Lake
Traditional Launch Cruises
QUEEN OF THE LAKE

Readying sailboats for a day on the water at Fell Foot Park,
with the quay at Lakeside behind.

Taking to the water at Fell Foot Park, in a hired rowing boat.

WELCOME TO YHA AMBLESIDE

The evening light at Waterhead was lucky, the swans too. The skill was just being there with camera at the ready.

MY WINDERMERE

When the Morrison family went on holiday, it was to the shores of Windermere. Under the benign influence of Arthur Ransome's *Swallows and Amazons*, we embraced the idea of water-based adventures. We dressed up as brigands and rowed across the lake to Pirate Island (though the unimaginitive cartographers at the Ordnance Survey insist on the more prosaic name of Ling Holme). We would storm the island and search for the buried treasure (generally a cigarette tin filled with sweets) that my Dad had buried a few days earlier.

Arthur Ransome had a profound effect on me: especially the idea of letting children sail boats in all weathers, without any kind of adult supervision or risk assessment, which these days would have Social Services making discreet enquiries. I followed the adventures of John, Susan, Roger and the provocatively named Titty. We didn't drown, so, according to Ransome's Darwinian motto, we obviously weren't duffers.

We swam, fished for perch, and watched wagtails pick their dainty way along the water's edge. We messed about in boats and skimmed flat stones across the water. At the end of the day we'd watch the sun go down over Coniston Old Man.

There was a time when the boatyards of Bowness were full of men in grubby overalls, with dirt under their fingernails, who actually built and repaired boats. These same boatyards were converted into smart salesrooms, full of sleek, sexy speedboats, and the men who worked there wore business suits. They sat at desks punching pocket calculators, and didn't need to wipe their hands on their overalls before shaking yours. Following the speed restrictions on the lake, the showrooms have changed yet again. Most of the speedboats have gone; you're more likely to see Fair Isle sweaters on sale these days, or novelty chess sets.

I can remember when you could barely buy a meal in Bowness. Visitors would wander morosely around the town, trying to get out of the rain. The Royalty cinema, at the top of Craig Brow, screened *The Sound of Music* every day for about

A couple of fishermen trying their luck near the island of Ling Holme.

twenty years. It's all different now. There is a bewildering variety of eateries in Bowness, and the Royalty boasts three screens. None of them shows *The Sound of Music*. Not to be outdone, Ambleside has two cinemas and some rather posh restaurants.

I remember, too, the hard winter of 1963, when the lake was frozen solid for weeks on end, except for a small strip of open water kept clear of ice by the ferry. With each crossing, thousands of birds would take off, and settle back on the water behind the ferry. Some birds were not so lucky: I saw swans and ducks frozen into the ice. At night the ice creaked and groaned alarmingly, as huge plates of ice ground against each other – plucking wooden piers and jetties from their foundations as though they were made of matchsticks.

People walked on the ice; some trusting souls even drove their cars across the lake, just to save on ferry tolls. I have skated – inelegantly – on the ice, and wonder when the opportunity will come again. The Lakeland peaks used to have snow on their tops for six months out of every year. But not any more. Some winters there's barely any snow at all.

Now that I am lucky enough to live by the lake, I realise that Windermere is a lake of many moods, whose character changes by the hour. Early mornings can be magical at any time of year, whether you're out on the water or enjoying the view from one of the surrounding fells. I have a dinghy with an electric motor; it may not be very powerful, but, then, I'm seldom in a hurry. It's a joy to be out on the lake when the only ripples are mine. The motor runs almost silently; some mornings, as I cruise across the glassy water, the loudest noise I can hear is the chattering of my teeth.

Early in the morning, the lake belongs to the birds. The water has an unusual transparency, before it is disturbed; it's like the world has been washed clean in the night. I seldom have the lake to myself for long. Char fishermen drift by at a similar funereal pace, followed by sailboats, canoes, kayaks, windsurfers, other dinghies and one or two of the expensive cruisers that seem to spend most of the time moored up in the marina. The lake would be overcrowded if more than five per cent of the boats were in use at any one time. But they're not.

Later in the day, when visitors are either making their way home, or ordering a starter in some upmarket Ambleside restaurant, the lake empties once again.

Boats at their moorings, between Lakeside and Fell Foot Park.

Sunshine and showers: my favourite weather forecast when I'm planning to take photographs.

This is another great time to be out on the water, to watch the bats in acrobatic flight and enjoy the sun setting over the Coniston hills.

If you look at the tourist brochures, and the souvenir postcards, you might get the impression that the skies over Windermere are always a deep and unclouded blue. In which case you'd be very, very wrong. The weather can be all four seasons in one day, which is why landscape photographers come here from all over the world. The light in the Lake District is always changing (unless you've taken a week's holiday, in which case the rain can fall without let-up for seven days straight, out of a sky of pewter grey). When I'm taking pictures my favourite forecast is 'changeable', and I don't feel as if I've had a proper day's photography unless I've been soaked at least twice.

The lake changes dramatically with the seasons. Springtime greens are fresh and vivid. Pleasure boats get a new coat of paint or varnish, as the tourist season starts. In 2007 the good people at the National Park were on the end of some good-natured joshing when, to avoid disappointing visitors hoping to see displays of Wordsworth's daffodils, they planted plastic blooms in Borran's Park.

Windermere in summer is benign. I've come to realise, over the years, that few activities in life are more relaxing than floating out in a small inflatable dinghy, being rocked by tiny waves. Distractions melt away; it's hard to bear a grudge, or think uncharitable thoughts, while the sun is shining and the swallows are twittering. In August, high summer, the water looks black, like molten tar. It looks to be all surface and no depth – a strange impression – like water reconstituted in a different, thixotropic form. When the sun goes down, it's a big red ball casting long, burnished reflections across the water.

Some people notice the first swallow of spring. But who sees the *last* swallow, dipping low over the lake, before its epic flight south? The biggest transformation to the lake takes place at the end of the summer season. The traffic jams melt away as the crowds subside. The dash for your cash doesn't seem quite so urgent; the pub landlords of Bowness might even crack a smile. The cognoscenti make a special trip at this time of year to enjoy

A self-portrait from the top of Wansfell, looking north to Red Screes and Kirkstone Pass.

the autumn colours. Talk of leaves turning 'brown' really doesn't do justice to a Lakeland autumn.

Hypnotically clear days – when you can stand on an outcrop and feel you could reach out a hand and touch the furthest hills – alternate with days when the mist clings to the lake. To be out on the lake when the mist is rising is a magical experience. The mist rolls in across the water, like smoke from a distant fire. Then, out of the mist you see a hint of the far shore: a mere suggestion, a patch of pencil shading. A yacht at its mooring appears out of the mist; you turn around a few seconds later and it's gone. A black headed gull chases its reflection and lands on the still water.

By the time winter rolls around, the lake looks altogether more primitive, more elemental. It takes very little imagination to see it as a prehistoric landscape. A heron takes off from the shallows, like a broken umbrella, and makes laboured progress across the water. Cormorants stand on rocks, like sentinels, hanging out their wings to dry. A pair of handsome ducks, red breasted mergansers, make a splash landing to jolt you out of your reverie. And if there are any birds that look as if they might have shared the skies with pterodactyls, millions of years ago, it's cormorants and herons and mergansers.

Some days in winter the water can be still and glassy, reflecting the frieze of Lakeland hills to the north. On other days – many other days – the lake reflects nothing more than the grey of a fretful winter sky. From a distance the lake can look to be made not of water but of slate or hammered tin or brushed aluminium. Suddenly the lake doesn't seem so benign. There's a life and death struggle out there, as an exhausted sailor clings with frozen fingers to the hull of his capsized boat. A pleasant day out on the lake has turned nasty. He'll have a tale to tell his family, once he turns his boat the right way up.

I've heard thunder reverberate around the lake like the roar of an Old Testament prophet. When the storm clouds gather over the lake, and the water is whipped up into white horses, Windermere can look very dramatic indeed. It's maybe then – when I'm huddled over the tripod, checking my camera settings – that I like Windermere best.

ABOVE
With barely a breath of wind to fill the sails, a yacht glides past Storrs Hall Hotel.

RIGHT ABOVE
Morning mist, almost setting the lake ablaze.

RIGHT BELOW
Yachts at their moorings on an autumn morning, the reflections vignetted by mist.

The River Leven flowing through the arches of Newby Bridge, towards its sandy estuary in Morecambe Bay.

A solitary sailboat and a sky the colour of a day-old bruise.

A typical landscape on the low-lying fells around Windermere: heathland and silver birches, with knuckles of rock pushing through the bracken.

Two canoeists meet on a misty day at the northern end of the lake.

Classic, elegant and wooden-hulled, 'Windermere' class yachts during a race.

ABOVE

The vivid greens of early summer: Lakeside and the River Leven from Gummer's How.

RIGHT

Sailing into the wind . . . shooting into the sun.

182

ABOVE

Another view of Wray Castle, from the vantage point of Latterbarrow.

LEFT

Sailing away from the weather and the Royal Windermere Yacht Club.

ABOVE

The view due east from Latterbarrow, looking across the lake to Calgarth Hall and Millerground.

RIGHT

A busy day on the lake, between Lakeside and Fell Foot Park.

BELOW

The gardens of Graythwaite Hall, towards the southern end of the lake, are open to the public.

RIGHT

Cycling is a good way to get around the lake, with plenty of quiet lanes to explore.

KENDAL 7
HEATHWAITE

Watching the boats go by from the flank of Gummer's How.

The view from the slopes of Wansfell: Ambleside, backed up by Loughrigg Fell and the Langdales.

FOLLOWING PAGES
Bare branches and a sunset of pastel colours, from the bay at Waterhead.

INDEX